How to Make Money With A Quiz Night

Glyn Williams

All Rights Reserved. No part of this publication may be reproduced in any form or by any means, including scanning, photocopying, or otherwise without prior written permission of the copyright holder. Copyright Glyn Williams & GD Publishing © 2013

Other Books by Glyn Williams

'Small Business Marketing' Series

21st Century Tactics by Glyn Williams

The 7 Deadly Sins of Advertising

Great Marketing Channels (Coming Soon)

Others

How to Make Money with A Quiz Night

Join Glyn's mailing list and read his business blog (http://bit.ly/glynblog) at for more great tips on marketing your business

Table of Contents

Introduction
The quiz phenomenon!
What you will need
The format
Setup and running of the quiz
How to get the business
The 4 Steps To Success
Sample Quizzes
Summary

Introduction

First of all thank you for buying this Book. I'm confident that you will find this useful in generating extra business for you.

If you already work in the entertainment industry then that's great, you'll be able to skip the chapter on equipment. If you are not currently in the entertainment business not then you will find everything you need to know within these pages to start a lucrative sideline in presenting quizzes in bars, restaurants and clubs in your part of the world.

I worked as a mobile entertainer for over 30 years. Playing music and having fun with people at birthday parties, weddings and also played in night clubs. That work is great at the weekend party nights of Friday and Saturday but finding work midweek is difficult. (With the possible exception of Thursdays) I needed more work than that and so set about devising a step by step system to generate some more income

I used the information within these pages to secure several quiz nights a week. That is all I wanted at the time and if I lost one then I just got another using the same method. You might want to fill every night with a quiz making you a full time professional! The choice is yours.

I've used this method time and time again. In reality the marketing aspect transfers well to any kind of business, it simply works.

Read the book and really get to know the information. Understand the quiz format that we give you completely so that when asked you know it and can speak confidently about it when telephoned by potential clients.

Follow the instructions to the letter and you can fill as many nights as you wish. Even if you don't want to work those nights you could farm them out to other entertainers in your area and take a commission from them. Don't be scared of getting too much work – you can always say no.

Anyone reading this may think that it's easy to do a quiz and it is. The trick involved is using psychology to make sure that you a) get the work in the first place and b) keep the work once you have it. The book will provide a step by step system on not only how to present the quiz but also how to sell it into venues and how to make sure it lasts and lasts making you secure money every week

With that, let's move on.

The Quiz Phenomenon!

All around the world today there are quizzes in every city town and village. They are good business for venues and they bring in the much needed drinking population to spend their hard earned cash behind the bar.

Midweek trade is limited and venues need to give extra value to the customer to bring them in. Big screen TV for football is one method but when there are no events to watch then they need something else.

That's where you come in. As a jackpot quiz host you have an interesting proposition to bring those customers in. You must remember that bringing people in the door to spend money is your job. You are not there to ego trip you are there to bring in money to the venue's cash till and if you can do this then the venue will pay you handsomely.

Generally speaking you can earn between £60 / $80 to £200 / $300 for doing a quiz night in your area. Using this method of the Jackpot Quiz you will earn more than your competitors because you provide a better service and get people drinking for longer. That's what the venue is employing you to do.

The two quizzes I would present were on Wednesday and Sunday evening in bars. The Sunday quiz paid me £95 ($130) when others are getting much less with more work involved. The Wednesday quiz is a pop quiz and I got £120 ($160) for this when others were lucky to get 50 – that's the sort of area I worked in price-wise But what do I do for the money?

I turn up at the venue at 8:45pm with 2 speakers, an amplifier, mixer and music source (I use a laptop) – I start the quiz at 9:15, finish at 10:30 and I'm home for 11pm – so for that few hours work that's what I get and I can get that any night of the week I choose.

What you will need

This is not a 'start for free' business. you will need some investment however it is minimal and much of it you can buy from eBay second hand.

As a minimum you will need the following equipment

PA Speakers X2
In a small venue you will get away with one or even none as some venues have their own in-house pa system.

Professional Amplifier
or you could buy powered speakers. Personally I don't recommend an all in one solution as when one thing goes wrong it all goes wrong

Microphone
Get a reasonable Microphone, forget those cheap ones, don't spend less than £50 if you go for a new one. You will regret it if you do

Mixer
you need a mixer to put your mic into and your music source. there are cheap on eBay

Music Source.
You could actually use your ipod if you wanted to do this really cheap but I'd recommend using a laptop with some kind of media played on there

Printer

You'll need a printer for the question sheets, some posters and table flyers.

Pens
Don't forget this! I did once and had to spend a frantic half hour driving to the nearest garage and buying out their entire biro stock!

A Voice
No good trying to do this if you are mute. :)

Graphic Designs
You need a poster designing A4 in size with a blank space that you can write things in. No need to worry about this now, you will see what it's for later on. Do not worry if you have no design flair, there are literally hundreds of designers on Fiverr.com that will do you one for $5

The Format

Ok, this is very important so pay attention. This chapter will tell you how the quiz works in practice.

The quiz is in 2 parts and costs the customers £1 or $1 to enter – you MUST charge an entry fee – this money not only goes into building the jackpot but it also psychologically forces people to stay for the quiz once they have paid as no one likes throwing money away. Remember that you are there to get beer sales and nothing more!

The whole thing is in two halves. The main quiz and the jackpot.

The Main Quiz consists of 25 questions and a tiebreaker

The jackpot has a qualifying question and then 5 questions to answer to win the top prize

The Main Quiz:

The choosing of the questions for the main quiz is very important. Every venu has a smart Alec who could potentially win every week. This is NOT good news for the rest of the punters – they must have the opportunity to beat the smart Alec or they won't come back.

I'm not going to supply you with questions in this book as the kind of questions will be different depending on where you are in the world. A question about the long running UK soap 'Coronation Street' would not go down well in New York for example.

There are a myriad of resources on the Internet that you can use for finding questions, you should write your own questions based on your country and locality. You will instinctively know what will work. Don't make the questions difficult - they should be relatively easy for a modest intelligence to know and some of them should be judgment call questions. It's very important that your entrants do not feel stupid.

Ideally each week you should have several punters getting points between 20 and 25 correct – also, when you collect the answer sheets you should be able to see that most of the punters have had a stab at 90% or more of the questions.

After a few weeks you will know if you have the level of questions right.

The prize for the main quiz is donated by the venue in the form of vouchers to be used behind the bar on either food or beverages. – three vouchers of £5 each is all that is needed. It wil help you if you can design the vouchers for them or they may already have some in place.

Important! The prize must be able to be used on its own. Do not let the venue give you a voucher that is say $5 off a meal that is usually $20 - that is not good enough. The winner should be able to go to the bar and spend that voucher on anything.

The Jackpot:

The jackpot is funded by the quiz entrance money apart from the first £50 which you stump up just in case it's won early on (highly unlikely). Don't worry about this as the entrance money will eventually cover it and the jackpot will not be won very often. I ran it once for six months without a win and had collected over £500 by the tie it was won.

After you have asked the 25 questions and the tie breaker for the main quiz you then ask a jackpot qualifying question. This question is usually outlandish and one that everyone has to guess. A 'nearest to' type question. It could be something like "how many pints of beer did this pub sell over the weekend" - you don't have to have an exact answer, just one that they can guess at. It must be a question that no-one could possibly get the correct answer by using a smartphone – the nearest to the correct answer gets a chance to play for the jackpot.

The actual jackpot questions are important too, these must be difficult. I often used the old 'Family Fortunes' game show approach– you asked 100 people these questions and you have 5 top answers – if your jackpot player gets all five top answers then they win the jackpot money. There are lots of sites on the net with these questions.

We will cover exactly how you present both the quiz and the jackpot in the next chapter.

So, That's the format of the quiz which takes about 1hr and 15 mins to do it totally – not a bad wage for that amount of work is it ;-)

Setup and Running of the Quiz

It's important that you understand this whole process before you approach a potential customer. This might seem back to front but you can't sell anything until you at least understand it.

With that let's get to the nuts and bolts of running the whole thing. This is very important and much of it is aimed at you keeping the work so make sure you do all of this. There is a certain psychology involved in all of this. Remember that you are there to generate beer sales. I can't stress this enough.

Arrive at the venue in plenty of time – 45 minutes before the quiz is to start should be sufficient.

Only take the equipment you need – speakers, amp, mixer, microphone and music source. You also need enough pens for your punters, question sheets etc. Don't overload your show with disco lights as you are taking up valuable customer space, try to be compact and fit on a single table.

On arrival immediately take your equipment and set up in the agreed spot. If there are customers occupying the space simply put your equipment there and go ask a senior member of staff to ask them to move. You need to make sure you are central and visible. If the venue is large and has their own pa system arrange in advance to plug into it so the whole place can hear you

Get the kit setup and begin to play some background music and then check that you have actually brought your questions! – it doesn't hurt to double check this before you relax.

In an ideal situation and with minimum of equipment it should take you no longer than 10 minutes to set up.

After this go and have a beer with the venue owner – chat about all things and get to know the guy – it's harder for them to fire you if you get on well together so make sure you do this every time you work there. Get to know all the staff by their first name and make sure that at least one behind the bar is playing along. tell the customers that it's the staff member they have to beat this week to look good.

About 15 minutes before the quiz is to start grab the microphone and announce that there is a pub quiz tonight starting in 10 minutes with a jackpot of £XX (always£$50 to start with). Tell them that it's just £2 to enter a team of up to 4 people and that anymore than four is a 1 point handicap to the team per extra person – this encourages tables of 5 or more to have 2 sheets.

Tell them that you will be walking around the place with the sheets in just a minute and then just play the music – music is important too – slow ballads or oldies are good – no banging tunes here – these people want to relax, chat and have fun.

Go grab a pint glass from behind the bar, stuff some pens in it and go around the pub selling sheets – just say to people "sorry to disturb you, were having a pub quiz tonight, how many sheets would you like" – always assume that they will enter and mostly they will.

After you've been around the pub go back to the microphone and give them a five minute warning that the quiz is starting soon and that if they don't have a sheet they can get one from you – tell them where in the pub you are located. Also remind them that they are playing for a possible £50 jackpot tonight.

2 minutes before you are due to start grab the microphone and say something like this. "Just a 2 minute warning folks and a little time to take you through the rules for any that haven't been here before. Please give yourself a team name at the top of the sheet – be as imaginative as you wish. You will see on the sheets that there are 25 lines on the left and 25 on the right – please duplicate your answers on both the left and the right of the sheet as half will returned for checking. The quiz is in 2 parts – firstly we ask 25 questions followed by a tie breaker. Then we ask a jackpot qualifier and the nearest answer to that question will be playing for tonight's jackpot of £XX by answering some further questions. Please note that any team spotted using a smartphone to google the answers will be disqualified! Ok, get your pens ready and your beer in and well get started in 2 minutes."

You then go through the questions. Repeat each question twice with about 30 seconds in between the question and the repeat, and then about 40 – 50 seconds between that and the next question. – These things need padding out.

It should take you 20 minutes to get through the first 13 questions – then you have a half time break of about 10 minutes and then the remaining 12 questions, a tiebreaker question in case more than one have the same score and the jackpot qualifying question.

In total this should have taken about 45 minutes.

Give the customers the opportunity of you repeating any questions asked – just ask over the microphone if there are any they want repeating – don't worry, they will yell out the question numbers.

At the end tell your punters to fold the sheet in half, rip it down the middle and to bring half to you. you'll use that half later on.

As they do this try to spot the one nearest to the jackpot question and put it aside. Count how many teams you should have by checking the money in and make sure you have all the sheets in before giving out the answers.

Then give out the answers – before you do tell your audience to cheer if they have it right with something like "Yeah Baby" and boo when wrong – get them to practice once first This should be fun!. And tell them to give themselves a tick for a correct answer and a cross for a wrong one.

Then go through the answers – there is no need to repeat the questions – just say things like "question seven – The river we were looking for was The Danube"

Giving the answers should take no more than 5 – 8 minutes, If anyone argues with your answers tell them your decision is final and that's that.

Tell them to add up their answers accurately and play a bit of music whilst they do so

Next you ask for some quiet. You're going to count down over the microphone from 25 – tell them when you get to their number to cheer – tell them that if they cheer before their number comes up you will tie them up with a wet kipper or something stupid – they will do it anyway but you'll know when its for real.

So you go "25 …..24 …..23 …." Etc till your winning team reveals itself.

Check there are no others with the same number and ask the wining team to bring up their sheet for checking – get your checking sheet out and check they're both the same and have indeed got the correct amount.

Give the winner a choice of 2 envelopes – one has 2 vouchers in for a fiver each and the other has one voucher in for a fiver. – that's the end of the main quiz

Then you get a round of applause for the winners and then announce the jackpot qualifying answer and the team that's going to play.

Get the whole team up to the front and explain what they have to do – get the team to nominate one team member for the answer giver and tell the rest of the pub they can yell out answers to help them if they want.

Ask the questions and write the answers down take your time and use some tension building mood music

Go through their answers one by one and give them an opportunity to change ONE answer

"I asked you this and you answered that"

Explain to them that you won't tell them which are right and which are wrong but you will tell them how many out of five they have correct – tell them this is because the questions will stay the same APART FROM ONE for next week.

Tell them if they have all five top answers correct that they will walk away with the jackpot – simple as that.

Check the answers

Tell them "you have …… (dramatic pause) …. X out of 5 correct"

Chances are they haven't won – tell them that they don't go empty handed and give them the second envelope with the vouchers in – if the main comp won a fiver then this is a tenner etc etc

Round of applause, plug for next weeks show 2 minutes of music and fade – then pack up and have a chat with the guvnor before you go – oh, and don't forget your wages for the night!

That's it – job done.

The next chapter is all about getting the business in the first place – very easy to do ;-)

How to get the business

Right – this is actually the easiest part believe it or not.

Most entertainers cant be bothered though – they expect the work to come looking for them and when it doesn't they blame the time of year, the competition, the weather or any other lame excuse to cover their reasons for not getting off their backside.

There is one plain fact in any business – you have to go and get it.

Thankfully there is a simple 4 step approach that you can use to generate any amount of work that you want.

Follow this system and you could fill every night of the week if you wanted to leave the weekend for the more lucrative work. But most can't be bothered to get it. That's why they never make the transition to full time; and that's why the ones that do get off their backsides find it so easy.

Right then - hopefully by now you've decided that you want the business. Before I take you through the steps needed to get the business you have to decide how much money you want for the gig.

I don't know what your area is like for pricing – In London you can command up to £500 for a wedding whilst in other areas you're lucky to get £120. Based on your area you need to decide what it's worth. do some research, call up some disco companies and ask what they charge

Most important though – don't ever undercharge, you will kick yourself for it later on. If the average wedding is £120 then you must charge £80 or more for your pub quiz nights. If the average wedding is £250 then you should be looking at £125 for a pub quiz. You can always negotiate and should be willing to so start higher. You might just get it!

So, when you've decided your worth go to the next chapter – the 4 steps to success!

The 4 Steps To Success

I can guarantee that if you follow the four steps outlined below you will have as much work as you want. When you get the work – if you want some more then just do it again.

Step One.

Grab your yellow pages or go on yell.com and look up bars and clubs in your area. It doesn't matter if the bars already have quizzes so you don't have to avoid any of them.

Make a note of 25 pubs and clubs in the area you wish to work – write down their addresses and telephone numbers.

Call every pub on your list and ask for the name of the licensee or manager – make a note of it. If they ask you why you are asking just tell them you are putting something together for the pubs of your area and it will be in the post in the next day or so.

If they ask what it is you are going to send just evade the question as best you can. – you're a DJ – make up some bullshit!

Step Two.

Send each one on your list the following letter and quiz format sheet – Make sure that there are no more than 2 sheets in total – the letter and the format. – Its advisable to have a letterhead and logo at the top also if you don't have one then buy one from fiverr.com

Note: do NOT email this, direct mail addressed individually still works over email. Send the letter in a bright green envelope with hand written name and address.

Dear (insert name here)

Get More Customers Into (Insert name of pub / club here)

I know how hard it is these days to turn a good profit and to keep your customers in your bar. What with the tax burden on alcohol and the sheer choice available.

I believe that I have a way to both increase the numbers of your customers and also the 'spend per head' of those you already have.

So what is it?

The Jackpot Quiz Night!

You may have tried these in the past but the chances are it wasn't approached with the customer's psychology in mind.

The entertainment format offered by (put your disco name here) is designed to get new customers into your venue and to keep the customers that are already there whilst also increasing their spend.

Your venue/bar/whatever (insert name of pub here) seems ripe for this kind of Promotion and we would love to help you attract more business.

I have attached a brief rundown of the quiz format and the way that we would be happy to work with you. If you decided to engage us here is what we would do for you.

- Provide you with A4 Posters and small complements slip type printouts to leave around the bar and tables.

- Conduct a Jackpot quiz with a starting jackpot of £50 which we will pay for when it's won.

- From time to time we will host 'special' quizzes which will have prizes such as DVD Players, or Hi Fi equipment etc.

- We will produce all the paperwork involved – quiz sheets, props etc etc

Please have a look at the enclosed rundown of the quiz and give it your consideration. I will call you personally in a day or so to see if we can do business together.

Yours Sincerely

Joe Bloggs

God knows Disco

Second sheet: ...

The Jackpot Format

The quiz we are offering is a general knowledge one. Pop quizzes may be popular however it's very easy for the local DJ to win every week and when that happens your usual customers get tired of losing.

Our quiz is in two parts. Firstly, the main part of the quiz is 25 questions and a tiebreaker.

The questions from the quiz are chosen very carefully so that no-one person can win week in and week out. Some rely on pure guesswork for example and they span all areas of knowledge.This formula is tested to work in any area of the country and on all intelligence levels. After all, no-one likes to think they are stupid.

You donate 3 vouchers worth £$5 each to be spent behind the bar in your venue. The main quiz winner gets to choose an envelope A or B – one had £5 in and one has £10 in. Whichever one is left goes to the jackpot player if they lose.

Next comes the Jackpot. Entry into the jackpot is by qualifying question – it is usually something outlandish that no-one could possibly know the correct answer and the nearest one to the answer gets the chance to play.

We then ask five simple questions and if they get all five correct then they get the jackpot – simple as that

The quiz costs the customer £$2 to enter – this is very important and helps to keep your customers inside the venue – drinking your beer. The quiz entrance money is used to build the jackpot which is capped when it gets to £$100.

After the limit is reached we then use the entrance money to buy special prizes for the main quiz such as DVD Players etc.

In total the quiz lasts around 75 minutes including a break in the middle of 10 minutes. Normally we would start at about 9:15 and finish at 10:30 - 10:45 and if they're still in your bar at 10:45 the chances are they will stay till the end.

That's our format and it works. I look forward to speaking to you soon

****

Step Three

Within 2 days of sending the letter you **must** telephone the licensee. Sales are all about following up

You must sound enthusiastic and you must sound as if you do this all the time – even if you don't . the magic words are SMILE BEFORE YOU DIAL!

Make sure you are talking to the right person

Open up with "Hello name, I sent you a letter a day or so ago about increasing your business with our Great Jackpot Pub Quiz – Just checking to see that you've received the letter"

If they have seen the letter and have read it, ask if they have had time to consider the idea – if they have then fine – take time to discuss with the licensee how you can help. If not tell them you'll call back tomorrow.

Below are some responses you may want to bear in mind before you call.

1) We've tried it before and it didn't work.

That's great – at least you've had a go with it, can you tell me why it failed?

LISTEN to the answer – no matter what the answer is say this "The quiz we do is tried and tested – it works and it really does increase business, I'm so confident

I could help you, would you be willing to have a trial for say four weeks just to see how it goes?

Try to get the sale… I can't hold your hand anymore than this

2) How much will it cost us?

If they say that then you're in – that's a definite buying signal.

Before you reveal the price you must go over with them what you will do. This is called building the sale - you have to make it sound like a no-brainer. Tell them about the posters, the jackpot prize (don't worry, it only gets won every blue moon), the small flyers the extra prizes as the jackpot builds. Before you give them a price ask which night they were thinking of. When they tell you rustle some paper and say 'just checking my diary'

If you're free for that night say' brilliant! – I can do that for you, the cost would normally be (your price plus £25) but I'm willing to do it myself on a trial basis for you for (£xx) to see how it goes. STRAIGHT AWAY SAY "when would you like to start" assume they will buy.

3) I'm Not interested

"Ok, no worries, keep us in mind if you have any other ideas you would like to try, Can I ask why?"

find out the real reason, it could be that you've called at a bad time, it could be that they already have a quiz night. Find out and make notes.

Try a final close "What would have to happen for you to consider this a strong possibility?" if the answer is "hell freezing over" then it's dead.

Number 3 is the one you will mostly get, **get used to people saying no.** what are they going to do – break your legs? No. – no's don't hurt, think that for every no you get you are getting closer to a yes – and here's a better way of thinking positive

Out of the 25 letters you should get 2 to 3 that say yes to a trial if nothing else – in a good unharvested area you will get 5 or 6 saying yes.. But for the sake of argument let's say you will only get one yes.

Let's say that you charge £80 for a quiz and on average it runs for 6 months before they tire of it (normally about 2 years in reality!)

So – you made 25 calls and got 24 no's but one yes

That one yes earned you a staggering £2080 over 6 months

To find the yes you had to find 24 no's

Divide 25 calls by the money and you find that each call earned you £83.40 – even when they said no!!!!! – How's that for a positive outlook when you're on the phone?

Step 4

Before the night – preferably at least a week before. Visit the venue and meet the owner.

- Discuss where you will set your kit up
- Give him the posters you have made
- Give him the table slips you have made and even hand some out
- If possible in front of the landlord have a chat with some of the customers telling them you are going to do a pub quiz – once you've done this and the landlord knows his punters know about it – he won't cancel at the last minute.

Lastly, do a good job – follow the format we've given you and you will do well and the pub will be happy.

Job Done.

Summary

That concludes this lucrative business. The format works and keeps you there for months. The four week trial is always extended because you have a jackpot now and the customers of the venue would not be happy if the venue canceled it.

You are giving both venue owner and venue customer what they want. The venue sells more beer and food and the customers are entertained

You will have to design some small flyers for the tables in the venue and some posters. Again if you are not very good at design then fiverr.com can help for very little outlay

Although I have spoken in this book about using 'family fortunes' for the jackpot you can change this. At one time I used five audio samples from the movies and to win the jackpot they had to identify the actor and the film. Let your imaginagion run wild in creating unique jackpot methods. The jackpot should be difficult, always five questions and always change just ONE of the five every week. That's how to build a jackpot.

After a while you may want to include a music round in the quiz. I used to do a little 'bits and pieces' part where I would play an edited music track made of 10 songs. questions 25 to 35 we the artists of those songs. This really worked well as it was now a pop quiz too!

That's it now – I've done my bit – the rest is up to you.

Feel free to email me anytime if you have any questions. My email is radioglyn@gmail.com

Good Luck!

Sample Quizzes

Here are some sample quizzes to give you an idea of what to use

1. Who plays the female lead in Kill Bill2? - UMA THURMAN

2. What's the bone of the upper arm called? – HUMOROUS

3. What instrument did Glenn Miller play? Trombone

4. Which TV detective was based in the Channel Isles?   Bergerac

5. What do Americans call what we know as an estate car? Station WAGON

6. TV Theme 1

7. What is the name for a maker of hats? – Milliner

8. Used in jewellery, what's the fossilised resin of pine trees called?   Amber

9. Which plant does the Colorado beetle most often attack ? Potato

10. On which Island was Napoleon born? (Corsica)

11. Lisa Scott-Lee, Faye Tozer and Claire Richards were the female members of which five-piece group that had fifteen top ten hits, including two number ones, between 1998 and 2001?

12. What is the national sport of Japan? (Sumo)

13. What was the name of the lord who prepared a report on the use of intelligence during the run up the the iraq war this week

14. What is a cross between a collie and a greyhound called? (Lurcher)

15. What was the Character name, played by Jim Carrey as a Pet Detective? (Ace Ventura)

16. On a darts board, what number is directly opposite No. 1? (19)

17. What was the Name of Philip Schoefields Gopher? (Gordon)

18. TV Theme 2

19. Harry Allen was Britains last what? (Hangman)

20. What's the registration number of Postman Pats Van ? (PAT 1)

21. What would you suffer from if you had dichromatic vision? COLOUR BLINDNESS

22. What is Iron Oxide more commonly referred to as? (Rust)

23. Which car manufacturers emblem is a Prancing Horse? (Ferrari)

24. What is Britain's tallest building? Canary Wharf

25. How many hoops are used in a game of croquet? (6)

Tiebreak:

Approximately 18 billion disposable nappies end up in landfills each year. How many years does it take to decompose one nappy (takes as long as 500 years to finally decompose.)

Jackpot

In 1998, Sony accidentally sold camcorders that had the technology to see through people's clothes. – how many did they actually sell? (700,000)

Jackpot

Family Fortunes

Family Fortunes top answer required

1 Name a nice way of saying someone is Fat?

2 Something a man does more than a woman

3 Name Something that may be seen inside or around a Castle"

4 Name something that might Visit You During the Night"

5 **Name something that comes in sevens?**

Jackpot

Family Fortunes

Family Fortunes top answer required

Name a nice way of saying someone is Fat?   (1. Chubby 2. Tubby   3. Cuddly   4. Plump   5. Voluptuous)

Something a man does more than a woman
1. Shaves   2. Goes to the Pub   3. Moans   4. Swears
5. Watches Sport

Name Something that may be seen inside or around a Castle"   1. Armour   2. Moat   3. Cannons   4. Drawbridge   5. Dungeon

Name something that might Visit You During the Night"   1. Burglar   2. Mouse   3. Santa   4. Ghost   5. Lover

Name something that comes in sevens?   Days of the week / Dwarfs / Deadly Sins / Year Itch / Wonders World

1. Which is the warmest sea ? (Red sea)

2. Which vegetable is also known as the eggplant? (Aubergine)

3. Which earl gave his name to a boxing award ? (Lonsdale)

4. What word describes people who can use either hand with equal ease? AMBIDEXTROUS

5. Who was Noggin the Nog's arch enemy? (Nogbad the bad)

6. Which country declared war on Britain & France in June 1940? (Italy)

7. tv theme 1

8. THE WORLDS LARGEST FRUIT IS CALLED THE LOVE FRUIT or the Coco de Mare, AND CAN WEIGH UP TO 50 POUNDS, which is the only Country it grows in? (Seychelles)

9. Which sport uses the lightest ball? - TABLE TENNIS

10. What is the name of the Shopkeeper in Open All Hours   Arkwright

11. Who was the first wife of King Henry VIII?
    CATHERINE Of Aragon

12. Which of the 7 dwarves was clean shaven?
    Dopey

13. Which two metals make brass?   Copper and Zinc

14. • Who did JOHN WILKES BOOTH assassinate? (Abraham Lincoln)

15. Other than the name of an eating House, What is the Star of India? - WORLDS LARGEST SAPPHIRE

16. • Now that Ronald Reagan is dead, how many US ex-presidents are still alive? (4) – Ford, Carter, Clinton and Daddy Bush)

17. Food – what is Monterey Jack?   A cheese

18. • When can you add two to eleven and get one as the correct answer (clock face)

19. The Watch Tower" is a magazine associated with which group?   JEHOVAH'S WITNESSES

20. What is the capital of Nepal ? (Kathmandu)

21. What's the name of Sir Paul McCartneys wife? (Heather Mills)

22. TV Theme 2

23. Holly Johnson was lead singer with which group? (Frankie Goes to Hollywood)

24 In the film Jurassic Park, the park is on an island off the coast of which country?   Costa Rica

25 Which metal is the best conductor of electricity? (Silver)

Tiebreaker

In August 1999, Lori Lynn Lomeli set a world record by spinning how many Hula Hoops at the same time (82)

Robert Wadlow is the tallest man recorded in history. He grew to be eight feet and eleven inches - how much did he weigh when he died in pounds

490

Jackpot

Family Fortunes

Family Fortunes top answer required

1 Name a nice way of saying someone is Fat?

2 Something a man does more than a woman

3 Name another word for a Storm

4 Name something that might Visit You During the Night"

5 **Name a Slang Term for a Dog"**

Jackpot

Family Fortunes

Family Fortunes top answer required

Name a nice way of saying someone is Fat? (
1. Chubby 2. Tubby 3. Cuddly 4. Plump 5. Voluptuous)

Something a man does more than a woman
1. Shaves 2. Goes to the Pub 3. Moans 4. Swears 5. Watches Sport

Name another word for a Storm   Hurricaine   Gale   Tornado   Blizzard   Typhoon

Name something that might Visit You During the Night" 1. Burglar 2. Mouse 3. Santa 4. Ghost 5. Lover

Name a Slang Term for a Dog" 1. Mutt 2. Pooch 3. Hound 4. Doggie 5 Bow Wow

About The Author

Glyn Williams was born in Derbyshire UK in 1963. His father, brother and late grandfather were all entrepreneurs and businessmen. For over 20 years worked in sales and marketing and as a radio personality until in 2012 he contracted 'High Grade Dysphonia', the closest you can get to vocal cancer. Laser surgery of the vocal chords followed which solved the problem but left him without his most basic sales tool in full working order.

Life with a diminished voice forced him to look at a new career that was not dependent on the use of the spoken word. In a change of career he became a writer in 2013 and decided to share his knowledge of sales and marketing through books. He has also been a highly respected foreign exchange currency speculator for 12 years.

He continues to live in Derbyshire England with his wife Daphne.

Other Books by Glyn Williams

'Small Business Marketing' Series

21st Century Tactics by Glyn Williams

The 7 Deadly Sins of Advertising

Great Marketing Channels (Coming Soon)

Others

How to Make Money with A Quiz Night

Join Glyn's mailing list and read his business blog (http://bit.ly/glynblog) at for more great tips on marketing your business

www.ingramcontent.com/pod-product-compliance
Lightning Source LLC
Chambersburg PA
CBHW071542170526
45166CB00004B/1512